SNOWBOARDING BLAST

# SNOWBOARD CROSS

by Cara Krenn

CAPSTONE PRESS
a capstone imprint

Published by Capstone Press, an imprint of Capstone
1710 Roe Crest Drive, North Mankato, Minnesota 56003
capstonepub.com



Library of Congress Cataloging-in-Publication Data is available on the Library of Congress website.
ISBN: 9798875255809 (hardcover)
ISBN: 9798875255755 (paperback)
ISBN: 9798875255762 (ebook PDF)

Summary: Snowboard cross riders speed down a course with the goal of being first across the finish line. Readers will learn about the skills riders need, how courses are set up, and the stars of these thrilling competitions.

Editorial Credits
Editor: Carrie Sheely; Designer: Hilary Wacholz; Media Researcher: Rebekah Hubstenberger; Production Specialist: Tori Abraham

Image Credits
Alamy: Zoonar GmbH, 12-13; Getty Images: Al Bello, 16, BEN STANSALL/AFP, 15, Cameron Spencer, 20, Clive Rose, 8-9, 10, David Ramos, 22-23, Ezra Shaw, 24-25, Ian Walton, 29, Kevork Djansezian, 26, Laurent Salino/Agence Zoom, 4-5, 6, 18-19, 27, Millo Moravski/Agence Zoom, 11, Steph Chambers, 14, Streeter Lecka, 21; Newscom: Patrick Steiner/ZUMAPRESS, 17; Shutterstock: Real Sports Photos, cover

Design Elements
Shutterstock: AlexanderTrou, kostins, Rosovskyi, SAI A.D.A, sergio34



Printed and bound in China. 006459

# TABLE OF CONTENTS



Words in **bold** are in the glossary.

CHAPTER 1

# DASH TO THE FINISH LINE

*Zoom!* Snowboarders speed down a hill. They fly over jumps and drops. One rider dashes ahead of the others. But the second-place rider is close behind.

The racers are close together as they speed around a turn. Then they fly over the last jump. The finish line is in sight! Who will cross it first?

# LET'S TALK SNOWBOARD CROSS!

**banked turn:** a turn that rises at an angle

**berm:** a wall of snow used for turns

**drop:** part of a course that drops down; riders fly off the drop's edge and land in a lower area

**jump:** part of a course that causes a racer to go up into the air

**rollers:** a series of small jumps

**steep:** an area of the course that rises steeply

**step-up:** a jump in which the landing is higher than the takeoff point

CHAPTER 2

# SPEED AND SUPER SKILLS

Snowboard cross is all about speed! Four to six riders get set at the starting gate. When the gate drops, they're off! They race down a big hill. The winner is whoever crosses the finish line first.

**FACT**

Snowboard cross is also called boardercross.

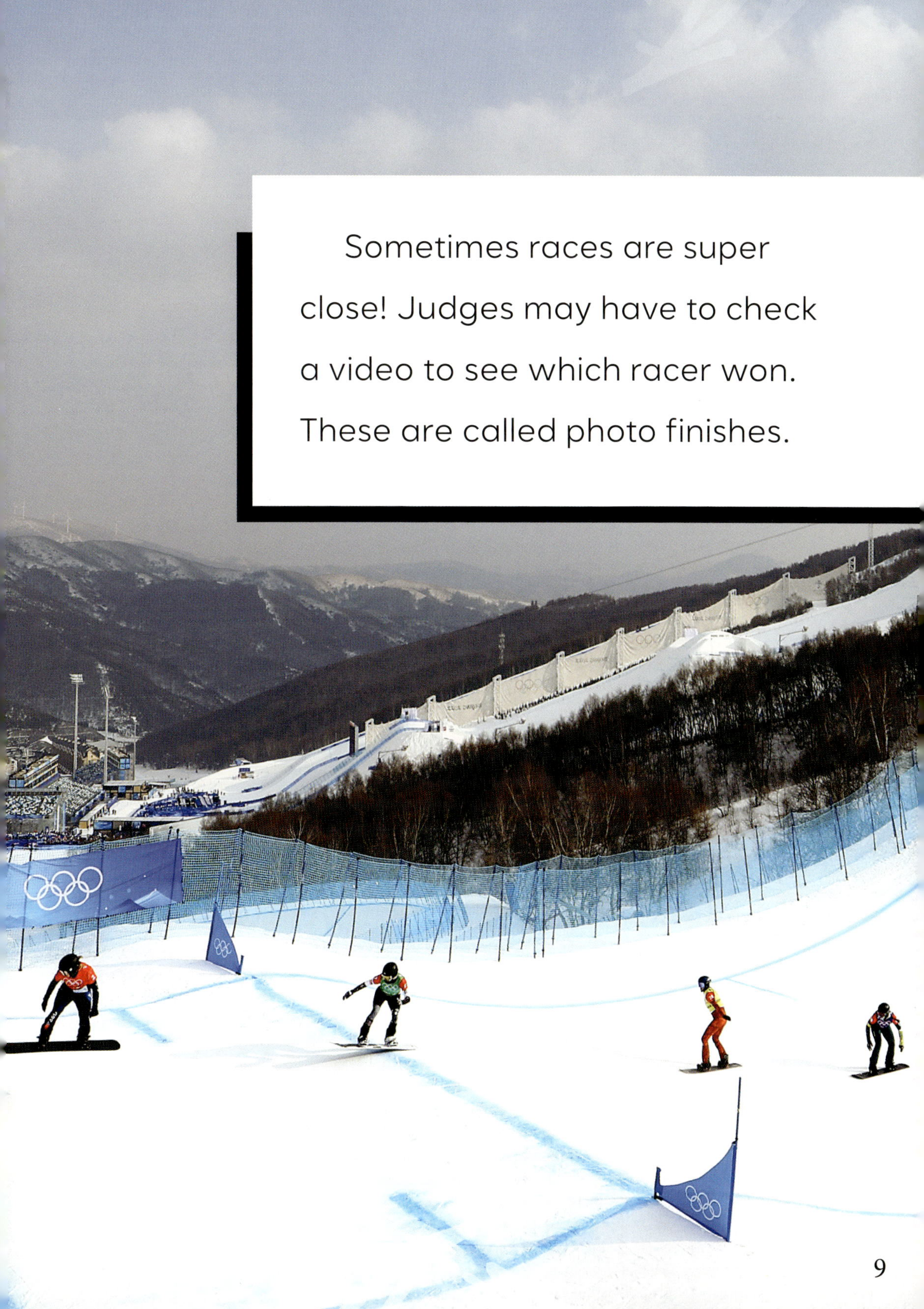

Sometimes races are super close! Judges may have to check a video to see which racer won. These are called photo finishes.

A snowboard cross course has many **obstacles**. Riders must be ready for anything! Riders fly over step-ups and drops. They speed over humps of snow and take hard turns. Each event has a different course design.

# WHAT'S ON THE COURSE?

rollers
step-down
rollers
banked turn

Crashes happen! Riders wear helmets and other gear to help them stay safe. They wear goggles to help them see.

Riders use a stiff board. It helps them stay **stable** while going fast. How fast do racers go? Super fast! They can reach speeds up to 60 miles (96 kilometers) per hour!

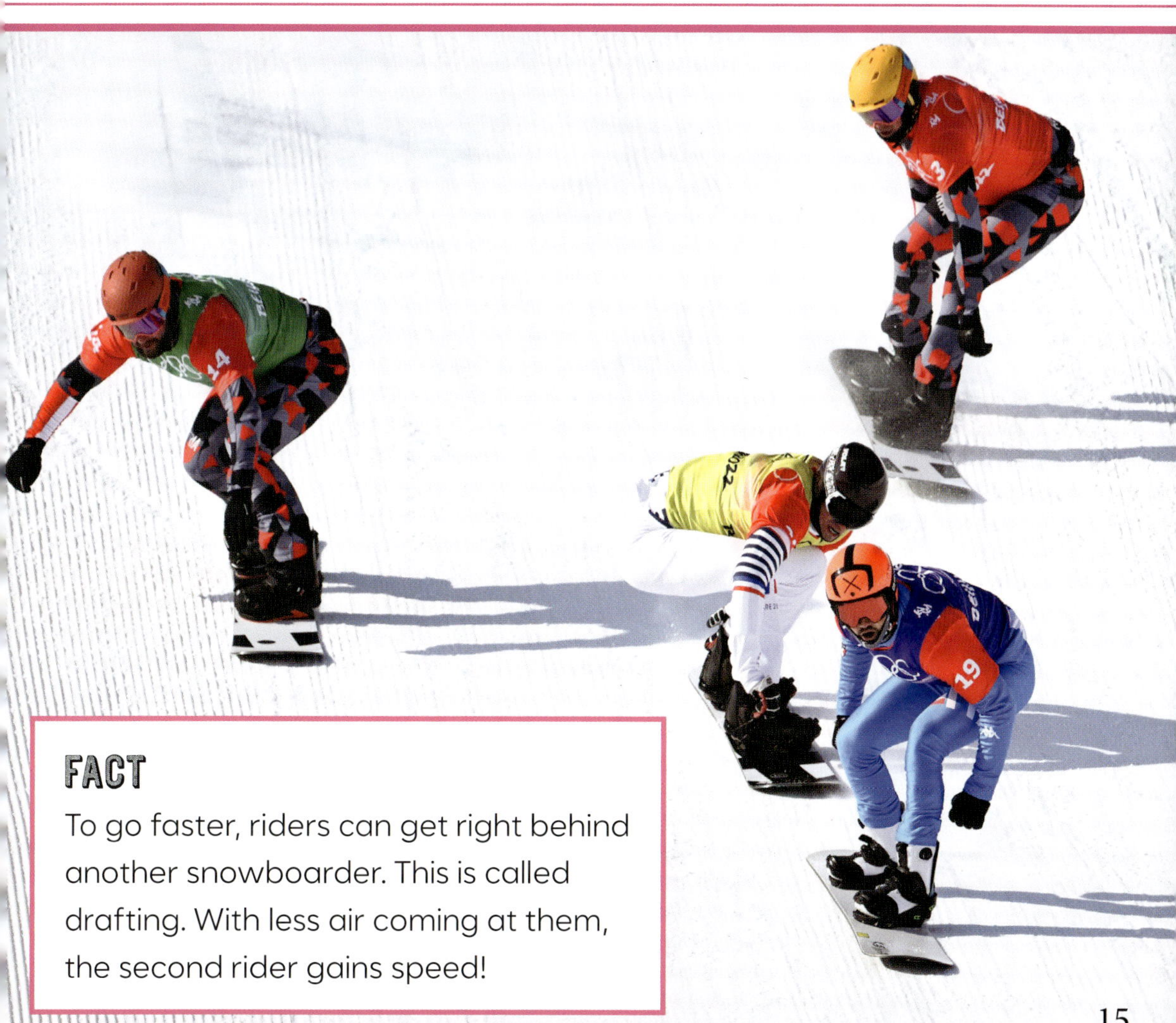

**FACT**

To go faster, riders can get right behind another snowboarder. This is called drafting. With less air coming at them, the second rider gains speed!

Snowboarders need a lot of skills. They must have great balance and control of their bodies. They learn when to stand up tall and bend down low.

Racers train hard. They need strong legs to take jumps and turns at high speeds. Racers need strong arms too. Racers use their arms to pull themselves out of the starting gate.

## CHAPTER 3

# TOP COMPETITIONS

Top competitions are the Winter Olympics, X Games, and the Snowboard Cross World Cup. Racers travel all over the world to compete for medals.

**FACT**

Snowboard cross became an Olympic sport in 2006. Seth Wescott was the first Olympic gold medal winner.

World Cup race

The Winter Olympics are held every four years. The X Games and the World Cup happen every year. The World Cup includes several races. The rider with the top **ranking** at the **season's** end wins the overall award.

Racers can compete in men's or women's events. They can also compete in mixed-team events. A mixed team has both men and women.

Mixed-team medalists of the 2022 Winter Olympics

**FACT**

In the Olympics, every racer wears a bib. The color of the bib shows the rank of the racer. The rider with the red bib gets to choose their starting gate first.

Racers first compete in **seeding** rounds. They race by themselves. Those with the fastest times get to choose the best starting gate. They have a higher ranking than other riders.

A rider in an Olympic seeding round

Next, riders compete in **heats**. They race against each other. The fastest racers keep moving on.

Then it's time for the final. The first person across the finish line wins the gold medal!

A semifinal heat of the 2025 World Championships

CHAPTER 4

# SNOWBOARD CROSS STARS

Lindsey Jacobellis is a famous American rider. She won every major snowboard cross competition. She won Olympic gold medals in both the individual and mixed-team events.

Lindsey Jacobellis competing at the 2022 Winter Olympics

Pierre Vaultier with his gold medal at the 2018 Winter Olympics

French rider Pierre Vaultier won Olympic gold medals in 2014 and 2018. He became only the second rider to win back-to-back gold medals in snowboard cross.

Seth Wescott won the Olympics twice for the U.S. He won 12 medals in the World Cup.

Seth Wescott after winning the gold medal at the 2010 Winter Olympics

Amy Purdy won three medals in the Paralympic Games. This major international competition is for athletes with **disabilities**.

Snowboard cross is filled with thrills. As the sport grows, new riders will become all-time greats.

SOCHI 2014
3
Amy Purdy

# GLOSSARY

**disability** (dis-uh-BI-luh-tee)—something that can limit people in what they can do, usually because of an illness, injury, or condition present at birth

**heat** (HEET)—one of several races where the outcome helps decide who will advance to the main event

**obstacle** (OB-stuh-kuhl)—an object a snowboarder jumps or rides over

**ranking** (RANGK-ing)—the position within a group

**season** (SEE-zuhn)—a part of the year where certain events or activities take place

**seeding** (SEED-ing)—the ranking of people in a competition

**stable** (STAY-buhl)—steady and staying level

# READ MORE

Berne, Emma Carlson. *Brenna Huckaby: Paralympic Snowboarding Champ*. North Mankato, MN: Capstone, 2021.

Herman, Gail. *What Are the Winter Olympics?* New York: Penguin Workshop, 2021.

Krenn, Cara. *Snowboard Half-Pipe.* North Mankato, MN: Capstone, 2026.

# INTERNET SITES

*Lindsey Jacobellis*
lindseyjacobellis.com

*Winter Olympics 101: Basics of Snowboard Cross*
nbcolympics.com/videos/winter-olympics-101-basics-snowboard-cross

*X Games: Past and Present Results*
xgames.com/past-results

# INDEX



# ABOUT THE AUTHOR

Cara Krenn writes children's books and for a variety of kids' magazines on topics ranging from trash trucks to magical creatures. She thinks a well-chosen book makes the perfect gift. Cara loves the beach, dance music, and morning walks with her cowardly dog. She is a graduate of the University of Notre Dame and lives in sunny San Diego with her husband, twin daughters, and son.